CW01512456

Original title:

Keen Branches Around the Fae Mole

Author: Paula Raudsepp

ISBN HARDBACK: 978-1-80559-370-6

ISBN PAPERBACK: 978-1-80559-869-5

Shaded Whispers of the Omniscient Grove

In the grove where shadows blend,
Ancient whispers softly send,
Leaves converse in gentle sighs,
Underneath the vast blue skies.

The sunlight dances on the ground,
Echoing each secret sound,
Branches sway in rhythmic grace,
Nature's pulse, a warm embrace.

Mossy carpets cradle feet,
Every path feels bittersweet,
Time stands still, yet flows like streams,
Cradled deep in nature's dreams.

Fingers trace the weathered bark,
Tales of life in every mark,
Breezes carry stories old,
In this haven, hearts unfold.

With each breath, the moment grows,
In the silence, wisdom flows,
Whispers shared by wind and tree,
In this grove, we come to be.

Chasing Glints in the Golden Leaves

In the breeze, they whisper low,
Golden leaves, in sunlight's glow.
Chasing glints that dance and sway,
Nature's art, come out to play.

Paths adorned in amber hue,
Each step brings a world anew.
Laughter echoes through the trees,
Carried softly on the breeze.

Footprints left, a tale to tell,
In this wood, where spirits dwell.
Underneath a swirling sky,
Golden leaves, oh how they fly.

Time stands still in this embrace,
Nature's magic fills the space.
With each glance, a spark of gold,
In this moment, life unfolds.

As the sun begins to fade,
Whispers of the day cascade.
Chasing glints till twilight's end,
In the leaves, our hearts transcend.

The Mossy Kingdom Awaits

In the shadows where green reigns,
Mossy carpets, soft like veins.
Whispers dwell in twilight's light,
The kingdom waits, a hidden sight.

Ancient trees with wisdom stored,
Nature's voice, an unseen lord.
Among the ferns, a secret dance,
In this realm, we take a chance.

Streams that giggle, rocks that smile,
Every corner, nature's style.
Mushrooms peek from woven grass,
Histories in echoes pass.

A gentle step, a quiet breath,
In mossy realms, we conquer death.
The air is thick with fragrant earth,
A kingdom rich in timeless worth.

In the heart of this green land,
Magic flows like grains of sand.
The mossy kingdom will entice,
A hidden world, beyond the slice.

Beneath the Canopy of Dreams

Underneath the leafy dome,
Whispers weave a tale of home.
Softly woven, stars may gleam,
In the night, we chase a dream.

Moonlight spills on gentle ground,
Nature's lullabies surround.
As the fireflies light the way,
We find magic in the sway.

Every shadow holds a spark,
A moment bright within the dark.
In this stillness, hopes ignite,
Beneath the canopy, pure delight.

When the dawn begins to break,
All our dreams, new paths we make.
With each breath, the world awakes,
In this space, no fear it takes.

Beneath the leaves, our spirits soar,
Where dreams align and hearts explore.
In the quiet, we connect,
This sacred ground, we all respect.

Tales from the Circle of Stones

In the circle, ancient tales,
Whispers carried on the gales.
Stones that guard the secrets old,
Stories waiting to be told.

Lichens drape in silent grace,
Each stone holds a sacred space.
Echoes of the past we hear,
In this circle, we feel near.

Fires crackle, shadows dance,
Time lost in a timeless trance.
Spirit guides from ages past,
Bind us close, a spell is cast.

With each heartbeat, tales unfurl,
Mysteries in the stones' swirl.
We share laughter, joy, and tears,
In the circle, we conquer fears.

From the depths of earth and sky,
Stories live, and never die.
In the stones, we find our home,
Tales that weave us, never roam.

Lanterns of the Misted Dusk

In the twilight, shadows crawl,
Whispers of evening softly call.
Glowing orbs in gentle hands,
Light the path where silence stands.

Breeze sweeps over tangled grass,
Flickering flames, a dance with class.
Stars above begin their sweep,
As night unveils her secrets deep.

With every step, a tale is spun,
Of dreams born out of setting sun.
Lanterns sway, a tender guide,
Leading souls on the riverside.

Footfalls dampened, hearts will sway,
To the tunes the night will play.
In the mist, a story brews,
Of love, loss, and hopeful views.

As lanterns promise to ignite,
The magic hidden in the night.
Fingers trace the air, divine,
In mystic dusk, our hearts entwine.

Echoes of Fragrance in the Flora

Amidst the blooms, a scent unfolds,
Whispers of nature, secrets told.
Petals soft as morning dew,
In colors bright, a vibrant hue.

Echoes dance on fragrant air,
Carried by winds without a care.
Every blossom tells a tale,
Of sunlit days and evening gale.

Honeyed notes and citrus bright,
Fill the soul with pure delight.
Beneath the sun, the colors stirred,
In blooming tales, a heart is heard.

Bees hum softly, nature's tune,
As flowers sway beneath the moon.
In gardens vast, our dreams we sow,
In fragrant echoes, love will grow.

Each breath taken, a memory sings,
As life awakens on gentle wings.
In every petal, a story's trace,
The fragrance lingers, a warm embrace.

The Fauna's Lullaby in Dappled Light

In the forest's heart, where shadows play,
The fauna sings at the close of day.
A lullaby soft in dappled light,
Bringing comfort to the coming night.

Rustling leaves, a gentle sound,
Nature's whispers all around.
Creatures stir, a soft parade,
As twilight blushes, fears allayed.

Crickets strum their nighttime song,
While owls hoot, where dreams belong.
The brook babbles, a soothing stream,
In the woods, a tranquil dream.

Frogs croak deep in marshy grounds,
While fireflies twirl in dizzy rounds.
Each note, a thread that binds the night,
In echoes soft, the world feels right.

As slumber wraps its tender shawl,
The wild whispers a soothing call.
In nature's arms, we quietly lay,
In fauna's lullaby, we drift away.

Beneath the Canopy: A Dreamer's Heart

Beneath the leaves, where shadows weave,
A dreamer's heart begins to believe.
In nature's cradle, hope takes flight,
As visions bloom and spark the night.

Golden rays pierce through the green,
Illuminating wonders seldom seen.
With every breath, a story grows,
Of hidden worlds, of ebb and flows.

The gentle rustle, a soft refrain,
Speaks of beauty and distant pain.
Each whispered wind, a secret shared,
In the quiet woods, the soul is bared.

Dappled light dances on the ground,
As whispers of aged trees abound.
Under the canopy, dreams convene,
A tapestry of what could be seen.

With every heartbeat, nature speaks,
To the dreamer's soul that gently seeks.
Beneath the leaves, in twilight's art,
Awake the visions of a brave heart.

Whispers Wrapped in Gossamer Threads

In the quiet of night, secrets sigh,
Gossamer threads float, twinkling by.
Moonlight dances on soft, silken dreams,
Whispers of wishes, or so it seems.

Fingers of fog brush the earth with grace,
Embracing the shadows, a tender embrace.
Echoes of laughter weave through the air,
A tapestry spun from stories laid bare.

Stars blink softly, nodding in tune,
Cradled in darkness beneath the moon.
Each shimmer a promise of hopes yet to be,
Silently woven in fates we can't see.

Time wraps around us like layers of lace,
Holding the moments, a sacred space.
Voices long gone breathe life in the night,
Their essence lives on, in whispers of light.

In twilight's warm glow, hearts intertwine,
Gossamer threads, a fate so divine.
Together we venture, on paths yet untread,
In the whispers of night, where dreams are bred.

The Forest's Heartbeat: Tender Pulses

Beneath the canopy where shadows play,
The forest awakens with dawn's first ray.
Leaves shimmer softly, a gentle embrace,
Whispers of nature, time's tender trace.

Moss carpets the ground, a plush, green bed,
While rivers murmur secrets long unsaid.
Roots intertwine, a languid dance,
Life pulses slowly, in nature's trance.

Birds serenade the rising light,
In harmony's tune, day conquers night.
Squirrels leap, chasing rays of gold,
In the forest's heart, stories unfold.

Sunbeams filter through branches so wide,
Cradling the dreams that the forest hides.
Each step taken is a heartbeat felt,
Where the ancient magic of life is dealt.

As shadows grow long, the evening sighs,
Fireflies weave tales beneath velvet skies.
In the forest's embrace, souls intertwine,
With every heartbeat, a rhythm divine.

Enchantment Weaved in Petal and Leaf

In gardens where sunlight kisses the ground,
Magic breathes softly, warmth all around.
Petals unfurl, their fragrance so sweet,
Nature's confetti, a delicate treat.

Vines twist and twirl, in playful delight,
Colors cascade in a dazzling sight.
Bees hum a tune as they flit through the air,
While butterflies dance without a care.

Each bloom holds a story, a whisper, a song,
Roots deep below, where dreams belong.
With every rustle, secrets are shared,
In the tapestry woven by those who dared.

Morning dew glistens like diamonds of yore,
Inviting the dawn with a soft, gentle roar.
In blossoms and leaves, magic does thrive,
A reminder of beauty, alive and alive.

At twilight's close, the colors fade slow,
Yet the heart of the garden continues to glow.
For in every petal, a dream caught in flight,
Enchantment is woven, throughout day and night.

Across the Bridge of Where Magic Lies

A bridge of dreams spans the azure skies,
Where whispers of wonder dance and arise.
Step lightly upon the enchanted beams,
For beyond lies the realm of wildest dreams.

Each plank is a story, where time intertwines,
With echoes of laughter, shifting designs.
Golden horizons, kissed by the sun,
Awaken the spirit; adventure's begun.

Clouds drift like thoughts, both gentle and bold,
Holding the treasures of memories told.
With every heartbeat, the magic grows bright,
As shadows retreat in the embrace of light.

The river below sings a soft lullaby,
Inviting the hearts that wander and fly.
In the twilight's embrace, all fears dissolve,
As the magic unfolds, and souls evolve.

Crossing this bridge, we leave pain behind,
Embracing the echoes that life has defined.
With courage ignited, we soar towards the high,
Across the bridge, where our spirits can fly.

Whispers in the Woodland Glade

In the glade where soft winds sigh,
Leaves murmur secrets from on high.
A dance of light through branches plays,
Nature's voice in gentle ways.

Beneath the boughs, the shadows creep,
While twilight sings; the world's asleep.
Each rustling leaf a tale unfolds,
Of ancient spirits brave and bold.

The brook hums softly, clear and bright,
Reflecting stars that crown the night.
Soft footfalls on a carpet green,
Whispers linger, barely seen.

Mossy stones and twisting vines,
Hold the dreams where magic shines.
The air is thick with scents divine,
Where every petal holds a sign.

In this realm, where moments blend,
Time whispers stories without end.
The woodland glade, a sacred space,
Invites the heart to find its place.

Secrets Beneath the Canopy

High above, the branches weave,
A tapestry that nature leaves.
In shadows cast, the whispers dwell,
Guarding tales they rarely tell.

Underneath the sprawling trees,
Gentle breezes stir the leaves.
In the damp earth, secrets hide,
Where only silence dares to bide.

Footprints trace along the path,
Following echoes of soft laughter.
By the stream where memories flow,
Mysteries wait, quiet and slow.

The forest breathes, alive with lore,
Every rustle hints at more.
Ferns unfurl in greens and golds,
Holding the treasures time enfolds.

Secrets linger, soft and light,
In the heart of woods at night.
The canopy, a timeless shroud,
Whispers softly, strong yet proud.

Shimmering Shadows of the Enchanted Grove

In twilight's glow, the shadows leap,
Dancing softly, secrets keep.
Glimmers dance on leaves that sway,
In the enchanted grove, they play.

Moonlight spills like silver threads,
Weaving dreams where starlight spreads.
In the quiet, magic stirs,
Whispers bright as evening blurs.

Every step upon this ground,
Feels like ancient tales unbound.
Forest creatures watch in awe,
The pull of magic, an unseen law.

Where ferns unfurl and blossoms bloom,
Each breath carries a hint of gloom.
Yet hope ignites with every sigh,
In this grove where visions lie.

Underneath the starlit skies,
Magic weaves through all that lies.
Shimmering shadows, sweet and bold,
Enchanted stories yet untold.

Where the Sylphs Dance at Dusk

In the dusk where daylight fades,
Sylphs appear in twilight glades.
Gleaming whispers fill the air,
As they twirl without a care.

With gentle laughter, they entwine,
Floating soft 'neath pine and vine.
Their laughter weaves through dusky light,
A serenade to end the night.

Wings of gossamer, fragile, bright,
Glide through shadows, stars igniting.
Moonbeams cast their silver glow,
As sylphs and night begin to flow.

Nature's breath a lullaby,
Softly echoes, low and high.
In their dance, the world stands still,
Magic lingers where hearts thrill.

As darkness wraps the grove in dreams,
The sylphs in laughter, twirl and gleam.
A moment caught, a glimpse of grace,
Where night unspools its soft embrace.

The Elegant Sway of Hidden Wings

In twilight's hush, they gently glide,
The shadows dance, where secrets bide.
A whisper soft, a wisp of grace,
They flutter near, yet leave no trace.

In silent realms, they grace the air,
With every move, a fleeting flare.
Their elegance, a fleeting dream,
A hidden world, a silent theme.

Yet when they pause, the stillness sings,
A serenade of hidden wings.
In twilight's glow, they find their way,
In magic moments, they softly sway.

With nature's brush, they paint the night,
Under the stars, they take their flight.
In every heart, their beauty clings,
The secret dance of hidden wings.

So let us gaze into the skies,
And wonder at the subtle ties.
For in the dark, their spirits play,
The elegant sway of hidden wings.

Constellations in Blades of Grass

Beneath the stars, a world unfolds,
In blades of grass, a story told.
Each glint and glimmer, softly shines,
A cosmos found in lines and signs.

With every breeze, the whispers flow,
The universe in green below.
A dance of leaves, a twinkling show,
In quiet night, the wonders grow.

The dewdrops form, like gems they gleam,
In nature's lap, we find our dream.
A tapestry of time and space,
Constellations in nature's grace.

Where crickets sing and fireflies dart,
A symphony that warms the heart.
In every fold, a tale unspun,
The grass reveals what's yet to come.

So lie beneath the vast expanse,
And let the stars invite your glance.
For in this field, a magic mass,
We find our dreams in blades of grass.

Echoes from the Gossamer Veil

In twilight's hush, the whispers cling,
Through silken strands, the shadows swing.
A veil so fine, it breathes the night,
With echoes soft, it wraps in light.

Where memories float on softest air,
And secrets dance, so light, so rare.
Each sigh a story, ancient, deep,
In gossamer dreams, our souls shall leap.

The stars above weave tales anew,
While silken threads in moonlight dew.
A haunting song, a delicate call,
In every echo, we rise and fall.

The past entwined, the future near,
In every flutter, love draws near.
The veil holds close our hope's appeal,
In echoes sweet, we learn to heal.

So listen close, to what's concealed,
In whispers soft, our fate revealed.
Through gossamer threads that freely sail,
We find our truth in each soft wail.

The Serpent's Embrace on the Breeze

A serpent glides on winds so light,
In spirals deep, it weaves the night.
With sinuous grace, it finds its song,
A harmony where shadows throng.

Upon the breeze, it twists and turns,
In every curl, a passion burns.
The night enfolds, a warm embrace,
As moonlight dances on its face.

In whispers sweet, the air will sigh,
With every movement, dreams comply.
The pulse of life, the heart's release,
In serpent's grasp, we find our peace.

Through every scale, a story flows,
Of ancient paths, where no one knows.
In twilight's hold, it roams and weaves,
An endless waltz beneath the leaves.

So catch a breath, and let it be,
The serpent's dance, wild and free.
On gentle currents, souls will ease,
In nature's arms, the tender breeze.

Threads of Magic in the Air

Whispers dance on breezes fair,
Glimmers of a world so rare.
Colors swirl in twilight's hue,
Enchanting hearts as day is through.

Starlight weaves through branches high,
Echoes of a lullaby.
Each note a droplet, soft and light,
Guiding dreams through velvet night.

Winds of wonder gently sigh,
Carrying secrets, passing by.
With every breath, a spell is cast,
A fleeting moment, pure and vast.

From shadows rise the sprites and fae,
In playful games, they steal away.
Joyful laughter fills the night,
As magic sparkles, pure, and bright.

So linger not in daylight's glare,
Find the threads of magic there.
In hidden corners of the night,
Embrace the wonder, feel the light.

The Hidden Path to Faeryland

Among the trees, a secret lies,
Where gentle whispers entice and rise.
A pathway soft with mossy beds,
Leads to dreams where magic treads.

Deeper still, the wildflowers bloom,
Painting the air with sweet perfume.
Each step is light, each breath, a dance,
In this realm of fantasy and chance.

Glowing orbs flit through the night,
Countless souls in pure delight.
With every glance, a story told,
Of timeless journeys, brave and bold.

The river sings with silver tune,
Bathing all beneath the moon.
Whispers weave through leaves so green,
In this enchantment, all is seen.

From shadows, magic weaves its spell,
In hidden paths where dreams compel.
So step with care and open wide,
To the faery realm where dreams abide.

A Glance at Moonlit Mysteries

Underneath the pale moon's glow,
Whispers of the night bestow.
Shadows dance on silver streams,
Softly cradling starry dreams.

With every beam that kisses earth,
A secret tale of love and mirth.
Lost within the twilight haze,
Mysteries spun in shimmered rays.

Silken threads of dew-kissed mist,
Caress the night with gentle twist.
Creatures peek from 'neath the ferns,
Curiosity in every turn.

Echoes call from distant glades,
Drawing hearts through moonlit shades.
A glance at wonders yet unseen,
In the whispers where dreams convene.

So linger long beneath the night,
Where shadows weave in silver light.
For in the gaze of Luna's eye,
The universe breathes a gentle sigh.

Where Dreams Melt into Reality

In the dawn where shadows play,
Dreams begin to fade away.
Whispers of the waking flight,
Blending day with fading night.

Colors swirl in morning's breath,
Kissing softly what was left.
Reality bends with the light,
As dreams take shape and take their flight.

With every heartbeat, magic flows,
Waking worlds in gentle throes.
A tapestry of thought and care,
Where hopes and visions dance in air.

Each moment weaves a thread so fine,
Connecting dreams, both yours and mine.
Through valleys deep and skies so vast,
We find our place in dreams amassed.

So chase the dawn, embrace the gleam,
Follow the trail of every dream.
For where dreams melt into sight,
Life's true magic sparkles bright.

Tales from the Secret Sylvan Beneath

In the hush where whispers dwell,
A secret tale, a shadowed spell.
Roots entwined in a silent dance,
Life unfolds in a fleeting glance.

Moss cloaks stones like a gentle sigh,
Beneath the boughs where moonbeams lie.
Echoes call from the deep embrace,
Every step reveals nature's face.

In twilight's arms, the stories weave,
Fragrant dreams that never leave.
Time stands still as stars take flight,
Here in the heart, all feels right.

Breezes carry the tales of old,
In every leaf, a memory told.
Nature's lore in whispers shared,
A world enchanted, forever bared.

So wander deep where wonders meet,
In the sylvan secret, feel the beat.
For here in shadows, life anew,
The tales are waiting, just for you.

Dreams in the Mossy Shadows

Beneath the arch where twilight glows,
Dreams drift softly where the moss grows.
Shadows whisper of ages past,
In hushed tones that forever last.

Ferns unfurl like hands in prayer,
Crickets sing their songs of air.
A tapestry of night unfolds,
In every rustle, a story told.

Velvet night wraps the world in grace,
While stars twinkle, find your place.
The trees sway gently, ancient kin,
Inviting you where dreams begin.

Softest sighs cling to the night,
Guiding you to a hidden light.
In the forest's heart, peace is found,
Lost in these dreams, forever unbound.

So close your eyes and drift away,
In mossy shadows, forever stay.
Embrace the whispers of the trees,
And dance with dreams upon the breeze.

The Enigma of the Forest's Heart

Deep within where shadows play,
Lies the forest's secret way.
A heart beats fierce, yet soft and shy,
Beneath the canopy of the sky.

In tangled roots, the stories dwell,
Of lives entwined, a magic spell.
Each rustling leaf, a mystery shared,
In the silence, souls have bared.

The moonlight paints in silver hues,
Creating paths for wandering views.
Every glance a riddle spun,
In the heart of woods, tales are won.

With gentle grace, the spirits roam,
Guiding lost ones safely home.
In every part, the echoes sing,
Of timeless songs that nature brings.

So heed the call of the ancient trees,
For in their midst, you find sweet peace.
The enigma waits, a gift to share,
In the forest's heart, love is rare.

Songs of the Hidden Tranquility

In hidden glades where silence reigns,
Songs of peace flow through the veins.
Gentle breezes hum their tunes,
As daylight fades and evening croons.

Underneath the canopy wide,
Soft reflections unite, abide.
Water's laughter in crystal streams,
Answers the heart's quiet dreams.

Stars peek through the leaves above,
Wrapping shadows in tender love.
Each moment, a whisper of hope,
In the forest's arms, we learn to cope.

Nestled deep within the green,
Is where our spirits find the unseen.
Harmony weaves through the night,
Embracing all with gentle light.

So come to rest where nature sings,
And feel the joy that harmony brings.
In the hidden tranquility, we'll find,
A place where souls are gently twined.

Shimmering Hues of the Night

Stars awaken in the dark,
Painting dreams with silver spark.
Moonlight dances in its flight,
Whispers secrets of the night.

Shadows play along the ground,
Echoes of the silence found.
Colors swirl in cosmic art,
Filling up the timeless heart.

Gentle breezes softly sigh,
Carrying a lullaby.
Nature's canvas, vast and deep,
Invites the weary soul to sleep.

In this calm, the world stands still,
Every moment begs to thrill.
The night unfolds its mystic scroll,
Embracing every wandering soul.

Glimmers fade, new dawn appears,
Chasing away the hidden fears.
Yet in dreams, those hues remain,
Shimmering softly, sweet refrain.

Stories Weaved in Twinkling Light

In the sky, the stories twine,
Every star a tale divine.
Whispered truths from ages past,
In their glow, we hold them fast.

Fables dance on midnight's breath,
Tales of life, and love, and death.
Each constellation holds a name,
Burning bright, yet not the same.

Threads of silver intertwine,
Binding fate with design so fine.
Across the dark, their voices call,
Echoes gently, one and all.

Woven dreams in timeless space,
Finding solace in each face.
With every blink, the stories flow,
Lighting paths where souls may go.

In the night, our hearts unite,
Finding joy in shared delight.
Every spark, a life entwined,
Stories cherished, souls aligned.

The Leafy Haven's Song

In the forest, shadows play,
Nature's song both bright and gay.
Leaves rustle in the gentle breeze,
Whispering secrets among the trees.

Morning sun with golden hue,
Kisses every drop of dew.
Singing birds in vibrant flight,
Celebrate the coming light.

Roots embrace the earth so strong,
Hold the tales of right and wrong.
In this haven, life transforms,
Beneath the sheltering forest norms.

Every branch a story weaves,
Of the magic that believes.
Colorful blooms that dare to rise,
Open wide to greet the skies.

As twilight drapes its velvet cloak,
Silent wonders softly poke.
In the chill, a harmony,
The leafy haven's melody.

Watchers of the Night Bloom

In velvet dark, the night unfolds,
Silent watchers, tales untold.
Blooming softly, petals bright,
Guardians of the quiet night.

Moonbeams kiss each delicate flower,
Awakening at midnight's hour.
Colors whisper, scents collide,
Nature's beauty, deep and wide.

Rustling leaves sing softly low,
Healing hearts in gentle flow.
Every blossom, dreams attract,
In their presence, no one lacks.

Stars lend light to every stem,
Crafting nature's diadem.
Silent witnesses they bring,
With the joy that night can sing.

As the world wraps in its rest,
Night's dear blooms are truly blessed.
With each glance, the heart finds room,
In the stillness, watchers bloom.

Whimsy Where the Ferns Sonnet

In a glade where shadows play,
Ferns dance softly with the breeze.
Sunbeams trickle through the fray,
Whispers weave among the trees.

A laughter shared by earth and sky,
Where dreams unfurl in tender light.
Curious creatures flit and fly,
Painting moments pure and bright.

Mossy carpets cradle fate,
As time meanders, slow and sweet.
Here, magic blooms as hearts await,
Adventure's pulse beneath our feet.

The fragrance of the forest sighs,
Each breath a promise, deep and wide.
With open hearts, we jest and rise,
In this whimsy, we abide.

So linger in this secret space,
Where ferns and laughter intertwine.
In the echoes of joy's embrace,
We find the threads that sparkle, shine.

Lanterns in Unseen Realms

Beneath the night's mysterious veil,
Lanterns flicker, whispers blend.
Stories linger in the pale,
Guiding dreams where shadows bend.

In unseen realms where secrets glow,
Wandering souls begin to dance.
A glow where lost moments flow,
In reverie, we find our chance.

The moon spills silver on the ground,
Each lantern holds a tale to share.
In this realm, enchantments found,
We drift through twilight's gentle air.

Embers of hope adorn the dark,
Illuminating pathways bright.
With every spark, igniting a spark,
We uncover magic in the night.

As lanterns guide the weary home,
Through unseen realms, we drift and twine.
In the glow, our hearts will roam,
Finding peace in every line.

The Portal Among the Blossoms

Amidst the blooms, a door appears,
A portal veiled in petals' grace.
With fragrant sighs, it draws us near,
Inviting us to a hidden place.

The colors burst, a vivid dream,
Where butterflies weave tales of yore.
In this garden's wondrous scheme,
Each blossom whispers, "Explore, explore!"

Sunlight dances in golden hues,
As laughter blooms beneath the sky.
In nature's quilt, we chase our muse,
Among the blossoms, spirits fly.

A tapestry of joy and bliss,
This portal holds our hearts and minds.
With every petal's tender kiss,
We leave behind what time unwinds.

So take my hand, let's walk anew,
Through blossoms bright, our spirits soar.
The portal leads us both to true,
A world of wonder to explore.

Elysian Echoes of the Woodland

In the woodland where echoes play,
Elysian whispers fill the air.
Each rustling leaf has much to say,
A gentle hymn, both wild and rare.

With every step upon the ground,
A symphony of life unfolds.
Nature's music, soft and profound,
With ancient tales that never grow old.

Sunlight weaves through branches high,
Casting shadows, forms anew.
In this realm where dreams comply,
We lose ourselves in visions, true.

The brook's sweet laughter twines with grace,
As fluffy clouds drift, soft and light.
In nature's arms, we find our place,
Wrapped in peace, both day and night.

So linger here, let time suspend,
In woodland whispers, we belong.
Elysian echoes, gently mend,
Our souls entwined, a timeless song.

Treading Lightly on Forbidden Paths

In shadows deep, we softly tread,
Where whispers curl and secrets spread.
With cautious steps, the heart will sway,
On trails where night conceals the day.

A moonlit glow, a fleeting glance,
Dare we embrace this mystic dance?
Each choice unfolds a different fate,
In twilight's grip, we contemplate.

Veils of curiosity abound,
In haunted woods, the lost are found.
The air is thick with dreams untold,
As longing warms the night so cold.

With every turn, temptation near,
The pulse of danger draws us here.
Yet in the midst of risk and thrill,
We choose to seek, we choose to feel.

The Soft Murmurs of Untold Tales

Beneath the stars, the stories wait,
In whispered breaths, they craft their fate.
Each sigh of twilight holds a key,
To worlds unseen, where hearts roam free.

Echoes dance in the evening air,
With gentle tunes beyond compare.
A garden blooms with voices frail,
That weave the fabric of the tale.

In every shadow, legends stir,
While silence wraps them soft, demure.
Together we sit, minds entwined,
In this embrace, the truth we find.

The softest murmurs call us near,
To hear the whispers crystal clear.
From ancient times, to dreams anew,
These tales unite me and you.

Petals Showering Down like Wishes

From cherry trees, the petals fall,
A gentle rain, a silent thrall.
Each one a wish, a dream in flight,
Carried on winds of soft twilight.

As colors blend in twilight's hue,
The world becomes a canvas true.
With open hearts, we stand and gaze,
Amidst the blooms of sunlit days.

Each flutter brings a hope anew,
In every petal, love shines through.
They drift and dance, a sweet ballet,
Reminders of the fleeting day.

We gather dreams from nature's hand,
And let our wishes softly stand.
A cascade bright, a moment's grace,
In petal showers, we find our place.

Where Silence Speaks to the Stars

In quiet nights, the cosmos glows,
With secrets only stillness knows.
Each star a voice, so bold, yet shy,
In whispered hues, they light the sky.

Among the twinkling, hearts enthralled,
Within the hush, our dreams are called.
A tapestry of light and dark,
Where souls can meet, ignite a spark.

The silence breathes, an ancient song,
In stillness lies where we belong.
Close your eyes and just believe,
The universe has much to weave.

In moments shared where thoughts take flight,
The stars align to hold us tight.
Together floating through the night,
Where silence speaks and feels just right.

The Portal of the Woodland Spirits

In the shade where shadows play,
Whispers weave through leaves of green,
Ancient trees beckon the stray,
Guardians of a realm unseen.

Echoes dance in twilight's glow,
With flickering lights that guide the way,
Through twisted roots where secrets flow,
To realms where spirits laugh and sway.

Misty trails invite the bold,
To step beyond what eyes can see,
Where stories of the past unfold,
In every breeze, a memory free.

Veils of silence often speak,
To those who listen with pure hearts,
Each rustling leaf, a tale unique,
In woodland magic, all are parts.

As dawn breaks with a gentle sigh,
The portal fades, yet hope remains,
For every wanderer knows why,
The spirit world forever reigns.

Curves and Twists of the Lost Path

Upon the pathway not so straight,
Winding like tales of old,
With each turn, we contemplate,
The truths that we long to hold.

Moss-covered stones mark the way,
Each step a choice to make anew,
In nature's dance, we drift and sway,
Finding the lost in what is true.

Branches arch like a guardian's embrace,
They shelter dreams that float and fledge,
In the quiet, we find our place,
As we tread the winding edge.

Whispers rise from the forest floor,
Speaking of those who walked before,
In every curve, a secret core,
Of paths once crossed, now evermore.

So journey deep through bends and breaks,
Embrace the mystery in the mist,
For each lost path a journey makes,
With echoes of the past in bliss.

Resonance of the Hidden Hollow

In the hollow where shadows blend,
Soft murmurs rise from earth's embrace,
Mysteries that the ancients send,
Into silence, a tender grace.

Crickets chirp a lullaby sweet,
While starlight flickers above the trees,
Nature's heartbeat, a gentle beat,
In the breeze, a whispered tease.

Hidden treasures lie below,
In roots that twist, in stones that shine,
Each heartbeat speaks of tales we know,
Resonance of a life divine.

Waves of echoes weave through time,
Awakening dreams from ages past,
The hidden hollow sings a rhyme,
In harmony, shadows are cast.

So linger soft in twilight's glow,
Where every breath brings forth a sigh,
In this sacred space, we grow,
Resonance of the earth's sweet cry.

Phantoms in the Mossy Vale

In the vale where phantoms tread,
Moss blankets tales both old and wise,
With every step, a whisper led,
From shadows where the stillness lies.

Wraiths of memory dance through air,
In twilight's serene, gentle fold,
Carrying burdens of despair,
And secrets that the nights have told.

Glimmers of light pierce the gloom,
Painting stories on the ground,
In the heart of the silent room,
The echoes of lost dreams are found.

Softly call the souls once known,
In the woods, their voices hum,
In every sigh, a fondness grown,
Phantoms linger, yet they come.

Here in the vale, embrace the night,
With courage as your guiding star,
For phantoms weave a tender light,
Reminding who we truly are.

Symphony of the Sprite's Refuge

In the glade where shadows play,
Whispers dance in light's soft sway.
Fleeting notes on zephyr's breath,
Joy entwined with thoughts of death.

Bubbles rise from streams of glass,
Echoed laughter as they pass.
Nature's harp in harmony,
Sings of love eternally.

Petals flutter, colors blend,
In the twilight, dreams ascend.
Fireflies twinkle, night ignites,
While the world sleeps, peace alights.

A serenade of softest tunes,
Cradled close beneath the moons.
Sprites in joyous reverie,
Mirth awakens memory.

As time drifts on like autumn leaves,
Magic weaves what heart believes.
In this haven, secrets swirl,
Life spins on in quiet twirl.

Echoes of the Forest Heart

Deep within the ancient trees,
Where the woodland whispers tease.
Echoes call from realms unseen,
Nature's pulse, a vibrant green.

Mossy carpets, soft and thick,
Pathways low where shadows flick.
Birdsong paints the azure skies,
Carving love where silence lies.

Rivers murmur secrets low,
Windswept stories flow and grow.
Every breeze, a gentle sigh,
Underneath the watchful eye.

In this realm of vibrant hue,
Nature breathes, belief rings true.
Every heartbeat, every sound,
In this sanctuary, found.

Let the forest guard its dreams,
Weaving life in endless streams.
Every leaf a tale to share,
In the heart of woodland prayer.

Luminance Among the Thistles

Amidst thorns and prickly leaves,
Beauty hides where no one grieves.
Cascading blooms in golden light,
Filling hearts with pure delight.

Every hue a story told,
Whispers sweet and brave and bold.
Luminance its silent song,
In the thistles, we belong.

Hummingbirds in vibrant flight,
Darting through the day's soft light.
Nature's dance, a vibrant throw,
Painting joys that softly glow.

Beauty grows where few would dare,
Strengthen souls, empower prayer.
In the thorny wilderness,
Life reveals its happiness.

From the shadows, brilliance breaks,
In the thistles, courage wakes.
Find your spark in tangled vines,
In the heart where hope still shines.

The Glimmering Burrow's Secret

Underneath the earth so deep,
Secrets in the silence creep.
A burrow glimmers, life unfolds,
Each hidden treasure, story told.

Shimmering gems in caverns bright,
Dancing softly in the night.
While the stars above gleam high,
Mystic whispers float and sigh.

In this hollow, shadows stream,
Holding fast to every dream.
Creatures venture, bold and small,
In the depths, they hear the call.

Roots entwined like lovers' hands,
Nurtured in these secret lands.
Life persists, a hidden song,
In the burrow, we belong.

Echoes of a vibrant past,
Memories that forever last.
To the glimmering depths we go,
Where the heartbeat starts to flow.

Whispers in the Woodland Grove

In the grove where silence reigns,
Gentle breezes carry names.
Fading echoes through the trees,
Whispers soft as honeyed bees.

Sunlight dapples on the ground,
In this space, peace can be found.
Leaves a-chatter, secrets told,
Nature's tales in hues of gold.

Footsteps light on mossy beds,
Where the soothing river spreads.
Crickets sing their night refrain,
Echoed softly, sweet and plain.

Ancient roots in shadows deep,
Guard the dreams the woodlands keep.
Time stands still, as if to say,
Here, my heart will always stay.

At dusk, the fireflies will dance,
Nature's stars, they weave a trance.
In the grove, we lose our way,
But find ourselves in night's soft sway.

Secrets of the Enchanted Glade

In the heart of twilight's glow,
Secrets whispered, soft and low.
Beneath the boughs so intertwined,
Magic lingers, unconfined.

Mossy stones hold ancient lore,
Mysteries behind each door.
Crimson flowers bloom and sigh,
While the night creeps slowly by.

Moonlight spills a silver sheen,
Glistening on the emerald scene.
Echoing laughter through the trees,
Stirred like leaves in gentle breeze.

In the glade where dreams are spun,
Every shadow hides the sun.
Dancing spirits in the night,
Filling hearts with pure delight.

Secrets woven in the air,
Whispers carried everywhere.
In this moment, time stands still,
As the heart learns how to feel.

Dance of the Twilight Sprites

When the sun dips low and fades,
Sprites emerge in gentle parades.
With a twirl and flicker bright,
They paint the dusk with purest light.

In the glimmer of the breeze,
Songs arise from swaying trees.
Delicate as a falling leaf,
They weave the night, a sweet relief.

Chasing shadows as they roam,
Finding magic far from home.
Glimmers spark like stars above,
Filling hearts with endless love.

Luminous in their playful flight,
Twilight sprites dance through the night.
Round and round, they spin with glee,
Mischief wrapped in harmony.

As dawn approaches, whispers fade,
In the light, their dreams are laid.
Yet within the heart they stay,
Guiding spirits on their way.

Shadows Beneath the Elder Tree

Beneath the branches, shadows play,
Holding secrets of the day.
Ancient roots in silence spread,
Dreams entwined where time has tread.

Whispers linger, soft and clear,
Echoes of the past draw near.
In this place of sacred ground,
Every heartbeat's lost, yet found.

Leaves above in twilight swirl,
Telling tales in every twirl.
Moonlight weaving through each limb,
Filling moments, slight and dim.

Where the elder stands so proud,
Guarding dreams beneath the shroud.
Time unfolds with gentle grace,
In its shade, we find our place.

The night unfolds, the stars align,
In this haven, hearts entwine.
Shadows cradle those who seek,
In their stillness, wise and meek.

Rhapsody of the Gathering Sky

Beneath the vast and endless blue,
Clouds mingle, weaving tales anew.
Whispers echo in the air,
As sunlight dances, bright and rare.

Golden hues begin to fade,
In twilight's hush, the night's parade.
Stars awaken, shy and bright,
They paint the canvas of the night.

Moonlight spills on fields below,
Awakening dreams that ebb and flow.
Nature's chorus, soft and clear,
Calls to the heart, drawing near.

Horizons blend in shades of grey,
As shadows stretch, they softly sway.
The world prepares for sleep's embrace,
In silence, we find our place.

A symphony of crickets sing,
While gentle breezes start to cling.
Each note a thread in night's great Loom,
Binding together the coming gloom.

Guardians of the Whispering Grove

In the heart where shadows play,
Ancient trees guard night and day.
Their branches weave a tapestry,
Whispers shared, a mystery.

Sunlight dapples through the green,
Casting shapes that dance and glean.
Every leaf a tale to tell,
In the grove where spirits dwell.

Mossy stones and hidden streams,
Hold the echoes of lost dreams.
Softly tread on earth so old,
Secrets hidden, waiting to unfold.

A deer steps softly, grace defined,
In this realm, all life entwined.
Guardians watch with watchful eyes,
Beneath the boundless, azure skies.

As twilight casts its gentle glow,
The grove ignites, a sacred show.
With each rustle and quiet sigh,
The whispers rise, they not reply.

Lurking Amidst the Foliage Shadows

In murky depths of emerald haze,
Figures flit in secret ways.
Eyes glimmer like distant stars,
As creatures peek from hidden bars.

Silence thickens, tension grows,
Every rustle hints at woes.
Nature's pulse, a lurking breath,
Whispers of life, or hints of death.

Shadows linger where light retreats,
Chilling winds bring whispered beats.
In the thicket, secrets form,
Where mystery brews, a hidden storm.

A fleeting glimpse; a sudden sound,
A fleeting shape glides from the ground.
Eerie calls crack the night's refrain,
Calling forth the wild untamed.

The moon peeks through a veil of leaves,
Casting shadows, where fear weaves.
Yet beauty rests in every bite,
A dance of darkness, woven light.

The Dance of Subtle Sprites

In the glen where willows sway,
Sprites emerge at end of day.
With laughter soft as summer rain,
They twirl and spin without a strain.

Glowing orbs in twilight's fold,
Stories in their movements told.
With every leap and playful dance,
They weave enchantment, spark a chance.

Fireflies join in glowing spree,
Illuminating wild glee.
In the cool, they beckon all,
To join the night's enchanting call.

Whispers laced in fragrant air,
Carry secrets from their lair.
They flicker like the stars above,
Delighting hearts with tales of love.

As dawn approaches, sprites take flight,
Dissolving like a dream of night.
Yet in the heart, their rhythms play,
A melody that won't decay.

Within the Burrows of Magic

In shadows deep, where whispers dwell,
An ancient tale begins to swell.
With roots that weave and secrets spun,
The dance of fate has just begun.

Rabbits dart with eyes aglow,
Through paths where moonlight dares to flow.
The earth remembers every sigh,
As dreams take flight and spirits fly.

A flicker found in hidden glades,
Beneath the boughs where silence fades.
A gentle pull of hidden charms,
Where nature lures with tender arms.

In tangled vines and flowers bright,
The essence glimmers in the night.
With every rustle, magic stirs,
In the embrace of woods and furs.

So venture forth, the bravest hearts,
To where the veil of wonder parts.
For in these burrows, tales untold,
Awaken dreams of magic bold.

Threads Twisted in the Twilight

As daylight wanes, the world transforms,
In hues of gold, the evening warms.
A tapestry of stars appears,
To weave the night with whispered fears.

The breeze carries a tune so sweet,
Where shadows and mysteries greet.
Time takes pause as moments blend,
In twilight's grasp, the paths descend.

A harvest moon, a sparkling thread,
Lights up the way where ancients tread.
The nightingale sings a soft refrain,
While secrets linger in the grain.

Through tangled woods, where echoes call,
The forest breathes, enthralling all.
With every step, the heartbeat grows,
Of twilight dances, life bestows.

So spin the yarns of muted light,
As darkness folds the day from sight.
Within this realm, where dreams ignite,
All threads are twisted in the night.

Moonlight's Embrace in Flora

In gardens kissed by silver beams,
The petals stir with secret dreams.
With every glow, the night unfolds,
A gentle touch, the moon beholds.

The blooms lean closer, whisper low,
In lullabies, where soft winds blow.
The secrets linger in the air,
As shadows dance with tender care.

A world alive with glowing sights,
Where stars entwine with fragrant nights.
In foliage deep, the magic plays,
In every hallowed nook it stays.

The dew drops glisten, nature's tears,
Reflecting tales through passing years.
Within this place of flora's grace,
The moonlight wraps in sweet embrace.

So wander here, where beauty thrives,
Where moonlit bliss forever drives.
In flora's heart, where wonders gleam,
The night unfolds a dreamer's dream.

The Secret Lair of Sylvan Dreams

In wooded depths, a secret lies,
Where ancient trees touch endless skies.
In silent glades, the fae convene,
Within their realm, all habits glean.

A crystal stream with waters rare,
Dances beneath the starlit air.
With each soft splash, the echoes sigh,
As time slips past and dreams comply.

The mossy beds, a haven sweet,
Invite the weary soul to seat.
With every rustle, tales unfold,
Of sylvan treasures, bright and bold.

In twilight's hush, a lantern glows,
As whispers weave where magic flows.
The sprites awaken, laughter shared,
In hidden realms, where none have dared.

So step inside, with heart aglow,
And let the forest's secrets flow.
For in this lair, both soft and grand,
The dreams of sylvan life withstand.

Beneath the Twisting Vines of Wonder

Beneath the vines, so lush and green,
Whispers carry, secrets unseen.
Petals dance in the soft, warm breeze,
Nature's symphony, meant to please.

Sunlight filters through leafy skins,
Magic lingers where joy begins.
Twisting paths lead hearts to roam,
In nature's embrace, we find our home.

A world alive with color and sound,
Beneath each vine, pure dreams abound.
Every shadow, a story unfurls,
In this hidden land, lost boys and girls.

The sky above, a canvas wide,
Where wishes float on a gentle tide.
With each step, the earth sings too,
A song of hope, forever true.

Beneath the vines, our spirits soar,
Finding magic on nature's floor.
In every petal, love's embrace,
Together we wander this sacred space.

The Hidden Realm of Mossy Dreams

In a world where shadows softly creep,
Mossy dreams in silence keep.
Whispers glide on the evening air,
In this realm, no burden or care.

Beneath ancient trees, roots entwine,
Glowing softly, secrets align.
Every stone holds a tale of old,
Of wondrous things yet to unfold.

The stream flows gently, a lullaby sweet,
Where heartbeats and nature's rhythm meet.
Here, nothing is lost, all is found,
In this hidden realm, love does abound.

Ferns sway lightly, painting the ground,
In twilight's embrace, peace is profound.
In every thicket, dreams take flight,
Guiding us softly into the night.

With every breath, a soft release,
Mossy dreams bring a sense of peace.
Hidden realms where spirits gleam,
Awakening hearts in gentle stream.

Echoes of the Twilight Treetops

At twilight's call, the whispers rise,
Echoes dancing through hazy skies.
Branches cradle the fading light,
As day surrenders to the night.

The treetops sway, a calming sight,
Each movement filled with pure delight.
In the silence, the heart takes heed,
Listening closely to nature's creed.

Stars awaken, a playful glow,
Guiding dreams where wild winds blow.
In the tangle of leaves, stories blend,
Of fleeting moments that never end.

Moonlit paths invite the bold,
In twilight's arms, treasures unfold.
Eager souls beneath tree's crown,
Kissing shadows that dance around.

Here, we linger, casting weight,
As echoes weave, connecting fate.
Treetops whisper, weaving dreams,
In twilight's gaze, a world redeems.

Luminous Spirits of the Leafy Realm

Luminous spirits, bright and clear,
Dance between the branches here.
In the leafy realm, they shimmer bright,
Illuminating the blanket of night.

The wind carries their joyful play,
Guiding wandering hearts along the way.
In this realm where shadows blend,
Friendships bloom and worries end.

Every leaf a lantern aglow,
Inviting us where magic flows.
With each flutter, a spark ignites,
In the hush of breath, pure delights.

Beneath the boughs, a safe embrace,
Luminous spirits hold their space.
Letting go of the weight we bear,
In nature's arms, we find repair.

As night descends, we gather near,
Wrapped in whispers, always clear.
In the leafy realm, love's refrain,
Luminous spirits dance, unchained.

Moonlit Murmurs of the Forest Dwellers

Underneath the silver light,
Whispers dance in soft delight.
Creatures stir, both shy and bold,
Letting secrets softly unfold.

Echoes flutter through the night,
As shadows weave in gentle flight.
Stars above wink down in glee,
Nature sings in harmony.

Mossy carpets greet the feet,
Every heartbeat feels the heat.
A lullaby on breezes spun,
As moonlit magic has begun.

Branches sway with tender grace,
While fireflies find their place.
In every nook, a tale is told,
Of ancient dreams and whispers old.

So linger here, embrace the glow,
Feel the pull of twilight's flow.
For in this realm where night bestowed,
The forest's heart forever glowed.

Fantasies in the Shade of Ancient Trees

Beneath the boughs where shadows play,
The world grows dim, yet bright and gay.
Each rustling leaf a whispered thought,
In woven dreams, visions caught.

Time stands still in this green glade,
Where youthful laughter's never frayed.
The sun spills gold through branches wide,
As secrets of the woods abide.

Squirrels chatter, birds take flight,
In their revelry, pure delight.
With every step on earthy floor,
Imagination starts to soar.

The ancient trees stand tall and wise,
Guardians of the earth and skies.
Their stories stretch from root to crown,
In every twist, a tale renowned.

So come and wander, lost in thought,
In nature's shade, all battles fought.
For in these woods, where dreams take place,
The heart finds peace in nature's grace.

Enchanted Breezes and Whispers of Time

A breeze caresses, cool and light,
Carrying whispers of the night.
Through tangled vines and flowers sweet,
Every breath feels like a treat.

Time drifts gently, slow and kind,
In every rustle, magic defined.
Moments linger in the air,
Fleeting glimpses of stories rare.

From dawn's embrace to dusk's deep glow,
Wildflowers dance, swaying slow.
With every flutter, tales unfold,
Of wandering hearts, both meek and bold.

The melody of leaves a song,
In the forest where we belong.
Embracing life with every sigh,
As stars adorn the endless sky.

So let the breezes guide your way,
To realms where night meets break of day.
For in the whispers of the trees,
You'll find the echoes of the seas.

Guardians of the Glimmering Underbrush

In the thickets, shadows roam,
Lurking softly, far from home.
A world of secrets waits in hiding,
Where the glimmers set the tide sliding.

Mysterious eyes blink from the dark,
Each flicker turning life to spark.
The underbrush, a maze of dreams,
Where everything is not as it seems.

Roots entwined like ancient lore,
Hold the stories of times before.
A rustle here, a shadow there,
Tales of wonder fill the air.

While the moon's glow lends a touch,
Of magic that we crave so much.
Every step reveals a way,
Through the night, the forest's play.

So heed the calls of sounds that beckon,
In the undergrowth lies connection.
Guardians waiting, wise and bold,
In the glimmer, watch the tales unfold.

Swaying in the Breaths of Nature

Leaves dance softly in the breeze,
Whispers of the emerald trees.
Nature's song, a gentle hum,
In the quiet, peace will come.

Wildflowers sway in sun's warm glow,
A vibrant carpet laid below.
Butterflies flutter, colors bright,
Creating beauty, pure delight.

Streams babble with a crystal sound,
In this haven, joy is found.
Mountains stand, so strong and grand,
Guardians of this timeless land.

Clouds drift lazily in the sky,
Painting wonders as they fly.
Inhale deeply, feel the earth,
In her arms, we find our worth.

Dusk descends, the stars awake,
A tranquil scene, no hearts to break.
In nature's breath, we find our peace,
In her bosom, worries cease.

The Songbird's Serenade at Dusk

As sunlight fades to twilight's blush,
A songbird calls in evening hush.
Her notes cascade, a sweet refrain,
Echoing soft like gentle rain.

With every trill, the night awakes,
A melody the silence breaks.
In branches high, she finds her throne,
A queen of dusk, all on her own.

The sky adorned in hues of gold,
Her serenade a tale retold.
Each note a whisper, soft yet clear,
Carried on breezes far and near.

A chorus rises, nature's choir,
In harmony, the world inspires.
With every sound, the heart takes flight,
In the embrace of coming night.

The songbird's heart, so wild and free,
Guides us through this reverie.
With each refrain, the magic grows,
In dusk's embrace, the spirit flows.

Vines Entwined in Sweet Serenity

In verdant depths, where shadows play,
Vines entwined in soft display.
A tapestry of life unfolds,
With whispers sweet, their mystery holds.

Through sunlight's touch and raindrop's kiss,
Each leaf a promise, each stem a bliss.
Climbing high on trees so proud,
Nature's beauty sings aloud.

In stillness wrapped, a world so dear,
A sanctuary, free from fear.
Birds alight upon the green,
In their gaze, a peaceful sheen.

Beneath the boughs, dreams softly weave,
A place where hearts can truly breathe.
In tangled roots, we find our way,
In nature's arms, we wish to stay.

Through seasons change, vines will endure,
Their gentle strength, forever pure.
In tranquil moments, love will grow,
In sweet serenity, our souls aglow.

Where Moonlight Meets the Undergrowth

A silver glow casts gentle light,
Upon the earth, a soothing sight.
Whispers of night charm the trees,
In this realm, the heart finds ease.

Dancing shadows, secrets spun,
In their embrace, we come undone.
The wildflowers glow in pale beams,
Awakening the night's sweet dreams.

The air is thick with nature's grace,
Where every creature finds its place.
Moonlight spills on the soft ground,
A sacred peace in silence found.

Beneath the stars, a story told,
Ancient secrets, brave and bold.
In the hush, we feel the pull,
Of magic moments, rich and full.

Nature sighs, a soft embrace,
In moonlit glow, we slow our pace.
The undergrowth hums a tune,
Where heart and earth remember June.

Intricate Paths of the Verdant Realm

In the green embrace of leaves so bright,
Whispers of secrets dance in the light.
Twisting trails where shadows play,
Guiding the wanderers who lose their way.

Footsteps soft on the mossy floor,
Every turn reveals something more.
A melody calls from the depths of the trees,
Inviting the hearts that float on the breeze.

Ferns unfurl in the morning dew,
Painting the world in vibrant hue.
Paths interlace like a woven dream,
Where nature and spirit blend and gleam.

Sunlight filters through branches wide,
Casting nets of gold as the day does glide.
In this realm, where each step is art,
One can truly feel the pulse of the heart.

So journey forth on this verdant quest,
Where the mind can wander, and the soul finds rest.
Among intricate paths, let your spirit soar,
In the embrace of the realm forevermore.

Mysterious Nooks in the Elderwood

Hidden within the ancient trees,
Whispers echo on the cool, crisp breeze.
Nooks where shadows silently dwell,
Holding the stories the forest will tell.

Twisted roots weave tales untold,
Crusted bark, weathered and bold.
Soft moss carpets the forest floor,
Inviting the seekers to explore once more.

A glimmer of light in a darkened glade,
Points to the magic the woodlands made.
Beneath the ferns, where fairies play,
The heart of the wild leads the way.

Gnarled branches reach out like hands,
Guarding the secrets of ancient lands.
Every nook holds a hidden delight,
Where dreams are born and take flight.

So linger awhile where the wild things roam,
In mysterious spaces that feel like home.
In the Elderwood's embrace, let your spirit twine,
Unravel the magic, discover the divine.

Luminescent Echoes of the Sylvan Fae

In twilight's hush, where stars begin,
The fae take flight with a twinkling grin.
Glow of moonlight on petals bright,
Weaves a tapestry of enchanting light.

Whispers of laughter through the night air,
Calling to those who wander with care.
Dewdrops shimmer like pearls on leaves,
Inviting the heart that truly believes.

A path of silver, soft and serene,
Guides wandering souls to the unseen.
Where echoes of magic dance and swirl,
In the heart of night, a vibrant pearl.

Flickering lanterns in a twilight grove,
Map the way for the ones who rove.
Each step brings visions, vivid and rare,
In the realm where faeries enchant the air.

So cherish the glow of this sylvan song,
Where the pulse of the wild pulls you along.
In luminescent echoes, let dreams ignite,
Dancing with fae 'neath the stars shining bright.

Beneath the Boughs of Enchantment

Beneath the boughs where shadows creep,
Lies a world where wonders sleep.
Glimmers of magic in every glance,
A realm where dreams take a bold chance.

Leaves weave stories in whispers low,
Telling the tales of long, long ago.
A gentle breeze brings the memories near,
Carried on trails where the heart feels clear.

Mushrooms sprout in a curious line,
In a dance of nature, sacred and divine.
Every nook holds enchantment's spell,
In places where silence and secrets dwell.

Branches entwined like lovers' hands,
Guard secrets held in these dreamlike lands.
With every step, feel the magic rise,
Beneath the boughs, beneath endless skies.

So wander here, where the wild things meet,
Let nature's whispers guide your feet.
In the enchantment of this sacred ground,
The essence of life will always be found.

Castles Found Among the Ferns

In the woods, where shadows play,
Castles rise in green array.
Mossy stones and twisted vines,
Whisper secrets of ancient times.

Sunlight dapples through the trees,
A gentle song upon the breeze.
Forgotten halls and crumbling walls,
Echo with the past's soft calls.

Ferns embrace each weathered stone,
Guarding tales of love once grown.
Wandering souls can hear the lark,
In this realm, where dreams embark.

The glimmering dew, a jeweled crown,
Drapes the fern in nature's gown.
Each petal holds a tale to share,
Of castles lost, yet always there.

So linger here, where silence reigns,
Among the ferns, the heart regains.
A sense of wonder, pure and free,
In castles found, we come to be.

Beneath the Glint of Sighing Stars

Beneath the sky, a canvas bright,
Stars are whispering soft and light.
Each twinkle carries dreams anew,
Guiding hearts with hope so true.

The night unfolds like a tender sheet,
Inviting souls to rest and meet.
In shadows deep, we find our way,
With each sigh, the night will sway.

Waves of silence roll like a tide,
Beneath the stars, where wishes hide.
A shimmering path leads softly on,
To where the heartbeats dance till dawn.

In bittersweet, gentle embrace,
We find solace in starry grace.
Each glint reveals what we hold dear,
A fleeting moment, crystal clear.

So close your eyes and breathe it in,
Beneath the stars, our hopes begin.
With every glint, our spirits rise,
In sighing nights beneath the skies.

Moonlit Roots: A Silent Gathering

Moonlight spills on the forest floor,
Where roots entwine forevermore.
Gathering softly, shadows dance,
In the stillness, souls enhance.

A gentle hush, the world awaits,
As nature weaves its silent fates.
In the dark, an echo stirs,
Whispering tales through bending furs.

Among the roots, we seek our place,
With every breath, we find our grace.
The night embraces, soft and deep,
In moonlit dreams, our secrets keep.

So close your eyes and feel the earth,
In silent gatherings, we find worth.
Heartbeats sync with nature's rhyme,
In the moonlight, there's no time.

Together here, beneath the trees,
We share our hopes upon the breeze.
In the night's embrace, we feel alive,
In moonlit roots, our spirits thrive.

Realm of the Ethereal Glint

In a realm where shadows gleam,
Ethereal glints awaken dreams.
With every breath, the magic stirs,
Unseen whispers, gentle purrs.

Clouds of twilight, soft and light,
Float like whispers in the night.
The silver moon, with graceful glow,
Guides the path we long to know.

Stars align in silent grace,
Creating patterns, sharing space.
Each twinkle leads us to the flow,
Of secrets kept, yet meant to show.

In this realm, our spirits glide,
Among the glints, we will abide.
With every step, the world shifts hue,
A dance of light, forever true.

So hold this magic close, my friend,
In the realm where dreams transcend.
The glimmering fate, a wondrous hint,
In the ethereal glint, our hearts imprint.

The Dappled Light of Forgotten Tales

In the forest's hush, a whisper calls,
Shadows dance where the sunlight falls.
Each leaf a story, bending light,
Old echoes linger, hidden from sight.

Time-seamed paths of mossy grace,
Olfactory tales in this sacred space.
The breeze carries laughter, faint and clear,
Cradled gently for those who hear.

Beneath the boughs, tales intertwine,
Myths of ages, forever enshrined.
In every glimmer, a moment unfurls,
A tapestry woven with whispers and pearls.

An oak stands tall, its heart laid bare,
Guarding the stories that linger there.
Weaving dreams in dappled light,
Echoes of history, a wondrous sight.

Forgotten tales in radiant hues,
Carried on winds like morning's dews.
In this serene land, time takes flight,
Under the boughs of dappled light.

Wanderings Through a Realm of Whimsy

In a meadow where the wildflowers grow,
Time drifts gently, ebbing slow.
Butterflies dance on a sunlit breeze,
Each moment is magic, meant to please.

Curious paths twist and turn,
Secrets of laughter, waiting to learn.
Beneath a sky of cobalt hue,
The world is alive, vibrant and new.

Talking trees share tales of delight,
Stars spun silver in the velvet night.
A bubbling brook sings soft refrain,
Echoes of joy in the gentle rain.

In this realm, imagination soars,
Through opened windows, endless doors.
Every step is a dance of chance,
Lost in the beauty, caught in the trance.

Wanderers find solace in this place,
Where whimsy thrives and dreams embrace.
In the heart of mirth, life feels sublime,
A place where stories conquer time.

The Tranquil Secrets of Sylvan Hollows

In sylvan hollows, where silence sings,
Nature cradles all her offerings.
Sunlight spills in a golden stream,
Whispers of peace in a tranquil dream.

Ferns unfurl in a gentle curve,
Guarding the secrets they deserve.
Moss-rimmed stones cradle stories untold,
In the embrace of the woods, pure and bold.

The rustle of leaves, a soft ballet,
Life dances along, come what may.
Gentle creatures flit in and out,
Painting the silence with soft, sweet doubt.

In each hidden nook, a treasure lies,
Bathed in serenity, beneath the skies.
The world fades away, wrapped in green,
Sylvan hollows, a haven serene.

Time stretches like shadows at dusk,
In these calm woods, where life is husk.
The tranquil secrets will never betray,
A gentle embrace at the end of the day.

Dreams Entwined in Gnarled Roots

Beneath the earth, where shadows creep,
Gnarled roots cradle dreams asleep.
Whispers of wishes, lost in the dark,
A tapestry woven with fate's fine spark.

In the quiet, the heartbeats blend,
Stories of old, waiting to mend.
Ancient wood, wise and deep,
Guarding the secrets the dreamers keep.

Leaves rustle softly, cradling night,
Nurtured by moonbeams, stealing light.
A world unfurls in the depths below,
Where dreams like seeds of longing grow.

In tangled embrace, hopes intertwine,
Each whisper a promise, a sacred sign.
With every breath, the roots grow strong,
Binding the dreams that linger long.

From darkness to dawn, threads of ascent,
In the gnarled roots, our spirits are lent.
Awakening life in the silent dew,
Together we rise, the old and the new.

www.ingramcontent.com/pod-product-compliance
Ingram Content Group UK Ltd.
Pitfield, Milton Keynes, MK11 3LW, UK
UKHW021443210125
4208UKWH00003B/83